# TREES

# TREES

# IVAN ANATTA

THE CHILD'S WORLD

# CONTENTS

No matter where you live, a tree probably lives nearby. Trees thrive in nearly every climate, from tropical jungles to snow-capped mountains. They are so common we often take them for granted. However, trees are among the largest, tallest, and oldest living things on Earth! What's more, they are vital to our very existence.

People depend on trees for many things. Their fruit provides us with food, and their wood supplies us with building materials. Paper, rubber, and even chewing gum are made from trees. Trees also provide us with something we cannot live without. Through a complex process called *photosynthesis*, they absorb carbon dioxide and release purified oxygen. Without trees, humans and most other animals could not breathe!

On the following pages are some of the world's most familiar and fascinating trees.

# SEQUOIA TREES

The sequoia tree is named for a man named Sequoia who invented the Cherokee alphabet. The sequoia is also known as the "big tree"—for good reason. Some sequoias weigh in at 12 million pounds and are over 300 feet tall! Only about 70 groves of sequoias exist today, each containing from 5 to 1,000 trees. Some of these trees have been alive for over 3,000 years. It would be difficult to find a birthday cake to hold that many candles! Resistant to fire and disease, most sequoias die only when they topple over because of their enormous size.

TARA OAKS ELEM.

# WILLOW TREES

Willow trees grow in more places than any other tree, thriving from cold polar regions to hot tropical jungles. New flowers bloom on willows every year in April or May. Bees make honey from these blossoms. Most willow leaves are green in the spring and summer, but turn bright yellow before falling off in the autumn. In England people use wood from willow trees to make bats for a popular game called cricket. Artificial limbs are also made from these trees. Captain Hook's arm might have come from willow wood!

# BAOBAB TREES

The baobab is an unusual tree that grows in Africa. Though it seldom grows over sixty feet tall, its trunk can be fifty feet wide. Surprisingly, the huge trunk contains mostly water, not wood! By storing water, baobab trees can survive long periods of drought. Another oddity of the baobab is its fruit. Over a foot long, the fruit has a mealy pulp and many seeds, like the inside of a pumpkin. People don't eat the baobab's fruit, because it tastes awful. Monkeys seem to like the taste, however, so the fruit is often called monkey bread.

# Bristlecone Pines

Bristlecone pines may be the only living organisms older than sequoias. Some are over 4,000 years old—making them the oldest living organisms on Earth! Bristlecone pines live so long because they grow on top of high mountains, where few harmful insects and germs exist. A bristlecone can survive even if most of its branches die. Ordinarily, the trees grow to be about twenty feet tall. At very high elevations, however, they grow only a few feet tall. Unlike other pine trees, the bristlecone has skinny, bristlelike prickles on each cone.

# OAK TREES

Imagine thinking of names for the over 500 different types of oak trees! The cork oak is one of the most interesting types. Bottle corks, shoe soles, and life preservers are made from its bark. The unique feature of all oak trees is their fruit, called *acorns*. Acorns are about the size of marbles. They are extremely hard and make great snacks for squirrels. Because the wood from an oak tree is very strong and rots slowly, it was once used to make ships. Today, people use the wood primarily for building furniture.

# MAPLE TREES

While the oak has 500 varieties, there are only about 100 different kinds of maple trees. The sugar maple is the most useful. We make furniture from its wood and maple syrup from its sap. All maple trees have five-lobed leaves like that displayed on the Canadian flag. Another unique feature of the maple is its fruit, called a *key*. Each key holds a pair of maple seeds. In late spring you've probably seen keys blowing in the wind like propellers. In autumn, maple trees are very colorful. Their leaves turn bright shades of yellow, red, or orange.

# Bonsai Trees

You will never see one of these trees growing in your backyard. Bonsai trees are not a species of tree. Instead, they are miniature plants specially grown in trays. Bonsai trees range from two inches to three feet in height. People prune the roots and branches to keep the trees small, an art that requires skill, time, and patience. Oriental peoples invented the technique to display their love and respect for nature by recreating the characteristics of large trees. If properly cared for, bonsai trees can live for hundreds of years!

# JOSHUA TREES

The Joshua tree is one of the few tree species that lives in the desert. Specialized leaves and bark prevent it from losing valuable moisture. The Joshua tree has white flowers that open in the evening. Attracted by the flowers' strong fragrance, moths come and pollinate them. Native Americans once made red dye from Joshua roots and used it to decorate baskets. The sweet flower buds made tasty treats for children. Today, very few Joshua trees remain. Most grow in California's Joshua National Forest, where the law protects them from harm.

# COCONUT PALMS

As you probably know, coconuts grow on coconut palm trees. However, coconuts on the tree look very different from those you see at the grocery store. What stores sell are just the seeds of the coconut. On the tree, the seeds are covered by tough, light-colored rinds. Some trees produce more than 100 coconuts each year. Interestingly, a coconut palm has no branches. Instead large, feather-shaped leaves simply grow out of the trunk. The large leaves are sometimes used to thatch rooftops. People also use them for making hats, mats, and baskets.

# Banyan Trees

You would have to travel to India to see a banyan tree. A banyan begins to develop when a bird drops a seed into the branches of another tree. The host tree then acts as a frame around which the banyan grows. Banyan seeds sprout downward, sending out aerial roots that eventually reach the ground. The banyan's roots and branches slowly smother the host tree. A single banyan can look like an entire forest! The branches create a large, sheltered canopy, where native merchants sometimes set up stands to sell their goods.

# SUMAC TREES

Sumac refers to a group of about 120 kinds of small trees or shrubs. During the summer, sumac leaves are dark green. Toward autumn, they turn brilliant shades of scarlet, orange, and purple. A young sumac's branches feel like velvet. But watch out—some of these trees are poisonous! Non-poisonous sumac trees produce erect clusters of red berries. Poison sumacs have hanging clusters of white berries. Smooth-leaved sumacs are another interesting variety. Some people make a tasty drink from smooth-leaved sumac berries.

# ASPEN TREES

There are two types of aspen trees—bigtooth aspens and quaking aspens. Bigtooth aspens have leaves with jagged edges that look like big teeth. Quaking aspens are named for the sound they make even in the gentlest breeze. In autumn, the leaves on both aspens change from green to brilliant yellow. Aspens have pale white bark that is softer than the bark of most trees. This soft bark provides little protection from insects, fire, or disease. In fact, most aspens begin to decay even before they are fully grown!

**PHOTO RESEARCH**

Charles Rotter/Archipelago Productions

**PHOTO CREDITS**

COMSTOCK/Townsend Dickinson: 7, 11, 19

COMSTOCK/William Ervin: 31

COMSTOCK/Art Gingert: 29

COMSTOCK/Russ Kinne: 17

COMSTOCK/George Lepp: front cover

COMSTOCK/Boyd Norton: 13

COMSTOCK/Michael Thompson: 21

E. R. Degginger: 9, 23

Michael George: 2, 4, 15

Robert and Linda Mitchell: 25, 27

Library of Congress Cataloging-in-Publication Data
Anatta, Ivan M., 1970-
Trees / by Ivan M. Anatta.
p.   cm.
Summary:  Describes the physical characteristics
and survival strategies of some of the world's
most interesting trees.
ISBN 1-56766-002-9
1. Trees--Juvenile literature.       [1. Trees.]       I. Title.
QK475.8.A49     1993                                        92-32286
582.16--dc20                                                    CIP
                                                                      AC

Distributed to schools and libraries in the United States by
ENCYCLOPAEDIA BRITANNICA EDUCATIONAL CORP.
310 South Michigan Avenue
Chicago, Illinois  60604